Kahuina Press

During my campaign for the Office of Hawaiian Affairs in 1984, Luther gave me this chant and translation:

E ala na moku	**Wake up!**
O ke kai lilo loa	**Our Islands are ebbing away**
E moe loa nei	**While you sleep**
Maka'e o ka po	**We are on the edge of darkness**

The reverend Abraham Akaka told me that these were the original words of Henry Opukaha'ia (1796—1818), one of the first Hawiian converts to Christianity.

Moanike'ala Akaka

Uncle Luther holds our four month old daughter, Hoʻoululahui Erika beneath the Christmas tree of 1975.

Holo Kūkū Me

(Galluping Along With)

Uncle Luther

99 Years of Hawaiian Rascality

Tomas Belsky & Moanike'ala Akaka

Acknowledgments

A grand mahalo to Stephen Paulmier for his generous friendship and computer expertise in making our portion of Luther's story real. Some portions of this collection were written decades ago and the original typists are now unsung heroes—but much appreciated. Special thanks to Cindy Taylor and Justin, and Adah Glasser for their typing contributions. Mahalo, too, for the memories and thoughts of Henry Biancini and of course to Eddie and Myrna Kamae for their support and contributions in research on Luther's early years. Finally a hearty Mahalo for the Aloha of the extended family of Uncle Luther.

Me Aloha Pumehana,

Tomas Belsky & Moanikeʻala Akaka

Dec. 1, 2014

First Printing 2015
ISBN-13: 978-1507500019
ISBN-10: 1507500017
copyright®2014
Kahuina Press
tomasbelsky@gmail.com
PO Box 1523
Hilo, Hawaiʻi 96721

Contents

Introduction i

Dancing Man of Hawai'i 1

Chazna Piva 7

Luther's Birthday 12

Hilo Quake 14

Cock Fight 20

A DAILY NEWSPAPER 26

Luther's Grandpa 32

Law and Order Luther 35

Uncle Luther Returns to Kaho'olawe 38

Hula Skirt 42

Red Luther 45

Pigs' Feet and *Poi* 50

Adventures with Luther 55

Last Round Up 67

Glossary of Hawaiian Words 71

Supplemental thoughts & images 73

Introduction

There was an article and picture that caught my attention in the Honolulu Advertiser from 1974, it featured an 89 year old Hawaiian man who was arrested for "rustling a cow". I told myself that I had to meet this man. His name was Luther Makekau. I met him several days later at a bar on Mamo Street. There was an immediate connection. As Hawaiian National Treasure Eddie Kamae said, "Luther was one of a kind!" Indeed he was—knowledgable about the old ways of our people; and a kolohe rascal and renegade that knew no bounds. I have to admit there were times I

wanted to "choke his neck." But, on the other hand, I have to say, Luther was a generous, unique and special individual. I remember the time he drew up a paper giving our daughter some land next to Hiʻilawe Waterfall in the back of Waipiʻo Valley. My father, whose grandfather had a rice mill and store in Waipiʻo Valley, went down to the Bureau of Conveyances to find that the land belonged to someone else. Pure Luther!

recalls Moanikeʻala

Who or even what is, was, Luther Makekau. In truth this has been the most challenging part of this book project. The entire collection of stories, and memories herein is an attempt to explain this unique Hawaiian man. This rough-riding cowboy became part of our family, and we shared the good times and bad with his unpredictability, tenderness, rage and pain. These recollections and notes of interest concern a very special friend a *kupuna*, a *kahuna* and a vast repository of things Hawaiian.

Uncle Luther 1890—1989, aka Tutu Luta, Kid Kolohe was born Luther Kahikili Worthington Makekau on Maui. In his 99 years of hard living, the modern history of Hawaiʻi transpired. Luther's life experiences range from being a student at Berkeley, California, a Parker Ranch Cowboy and to numerous short spells in local jails, usually for over-indulging in celebratory libations, cattle rustling and/or disorderly conduct. But Luther was also the Hawaiian man who would give, literally, the shirt off his back to total strangers, and be the guide for interested parties to hidden corners of the Islands, rich in lore and history. Makekau was an acknowledged archive of information on native plants, their uses in medicine, and how to locate, nurture and utilize them. His knowledge of the Hawaiian language culture and lore was profound and much respected. As a musician he played and danced with the best of his time, and his theatricality was legendary. Blest with exceedingly good looks and a seemingly inexhaustible supply of energy, he wooed and won many a fair *wahine* (female) throughout his entire lifetime—frequently to the dismay of disgruntled male suitors. In moments of impetuosity he is said to have ridden his horse into a restaurant in Waimea many years ago, and again in Pahoa in the early eighties. "I would like to be remembered as a Lover," he said, "but also as a rustler and a rough Jack." Luther roared well into his nineties. He will also be remembered, among other things, as a cowboy capable of mysterious communications with horses, a policeman, a moon-shiner, a mythical raconteur and an unforgettable segment of Hawaiian history. He died in Hilo at 99 years, it is said, making a pass at his last nurse.

Fascinaton is the simplest term that comes to mind when thinking of Luther. I seem to be somehow linked to this wild Hawaiian in a way that often puzzles me even now twenty-five years after his passing into that great unknown. Before I ever had any notion of visiting Hawaii (back in the sixties and early seventies) I was doodling sketches that somehow repeatedly looked like a cowboy. Being a Jersey lad, I wondered about such mental meanderings, but I just winked at it all and carried on. Then one day I met the lanky old cowboy in a bar in Hilo and kind of fell into a reverie of *déjà vu*.

The best introduction to Luther is the excellent documentary by Eddie and Myrna Kamae *Luther Kahikili Makekau—One Kine Hawaiian Man*, part of the Kamae Hawaiian Legacy Series, available everywhere in this age of magic. My observations and adventures with Luther are very personal and may well contradict some of the ideas held by others who knew him well. Explaining Luther is like trying to hold an eel hooked on your fish line: You find yourself with slimy hands holding nothing of real substance, although you know you had a grip on him an instant before. And you stand amazed as it slithers away into murky waters.

As a student of American History I see Luther Kahikili Makekau as a product of the American Experiment—an offshoot of both Manifest Destiny and the power of modern technology, propaganda and the cultural collision of East and West and Polynesia—with Hawai'i right in the middle of it all—with perhaps more to flavor the mix than most anticipated. I remember my astonishment when I heard Luther refer to another Hawaiian in a deprecating manner, and himself as "a Maori, and a thin-lipped Lover." And my thinking at the time, *where the hell does this twisted attitude come from?* And history gives me some of the clues needed to understand—not only Luther, but also Hawai'i and too, America and this crazy world we inherit from our parents and predecessors.

Dancing Man of Hawai'i

(1975)

I met an 85-year-old Hawaiian Man
a man tossed across the chasms of History
through no desire on his part
nor on the part of his people.
It is not fair to say
that a man is his people, but
is it not equally unfair to say he is not?
So, Luther Kahikili Makekau is Hawaii
and Hawai'i is Uncle Luther.
A man, an island
consumed by the great tide
pressed down upon a gentle, noble people
"noble savages" as the great philosophers
liked to call them.
One still sees signs of those days past
in the style of those who walk
the rain filled nights of Hilo.

But where is the language?
where the ancient gods?
and why is the dancing man crying?
Has something unthinkable

stripped away the music?
torn out the soul
of those who graciously opened their arms
coffers and hearts
to the newcomers?

What is the true religion of these newcomers?
Do they seek souls to save?
Fortunes to amass?
"Clothe and cover them up
Shame and redeem them.
Souls are saved through love"
they said, as they took the lands away.
Now and again you see them
old, tired, gentle, noble savages
destitute, landless Hawaiians in Hawaii.

And here we are today
two hundred years hence
a handful of brave dedicated Hawaiians
fight for the land, for the future,
for the children
and still they love.
Who would dare take what is offered
and steal the rest?
Ask an old Hawaiian
ask Luther
eighty-five years those eyes have flashed
watching fisherman become busboy
sister become prostitute

Elua

strange man rich
local man poor
changing land
changing spirit.
The *Aloha* chokes in the throat
as fertile valleys and families of farmers are bulldozed
making room, making room always
for progress and profit.
Profit and progress.
Take away the profit motive and
where are we?

Luther saw all this
as I see him in the bar
his bare feet (dancing man's feet)
raised above the bar-top.
"Luta! Get you feets on de floor please,"
the bartender could no longer pretend there
were no "feets" on the bar top.
His hat of straw at a rakish tilt
the words flow for the upteenth time,
"A lover, a killer and a cattle rustler
I've seen em all
I've been em all
but I'd like best to be remembered
as a Lover."

It came to pass
Luther was jailed for disorderly conduct
he wore my shoes those ten days in jail

Ekolu

do you wonder why I write of Luther?
Shall I say he is both king and peasant?
Dancing man and Sage?
The people versus Luther Kahikili Makekau
"Ten days dancing man," ordered the judge
that'll teach you to be disorderly.
So they took him, in my shoes,
and put him in jail.
And in jail
lover, killer, king of the rustlers observes
whose face presses close the cold steel?
The rich man?
The working man?
The poor man?
The dancing man sees all.

Sorry, Luther,
my words fail to hold you
you are the poem
a tribute and a haunting reminder
that the last scene to this drama in paradise
is yet to be played.
"Ua mau ke ea o ka ʻAina i ka Pono"
The life of the land is perpetuated in Righteousness.
"Love the land, for she is your mother"
a ten-year-old in a ghetto told me that.
"It is neither proper nor fitting that an island . . ."
Can you hear Jefferson rattling the saber in the closet?
"Ua mau ke ea o ka ʻAina i ka Pono."
Tea party talk

Eha

Uncle Luther with your tired frame
and blazing spirit
with your *kahuna* eyes
lead the way
Dancing Man in the borrowed shoes
Noble Savage of the Space Age
lover, killer, king of the rustlers.
O Dancing Man of Hawai'i
Gather about you
The spirit of your people
for I see the great ones in your eyes.
Bring music to their parched souls
bring rhythm to their blues.
Dancing Man
Dancing Woman of Hawai'i
"Ua mau ke ea o ka 'Aina i ka Pono."

EH LUTA! CAN GET YOU´ FEETS OFFA DA BAH, PLEEZE?

Eono

Chazna Piva

It was Ron and me that Luther claimed for his "sons"; but for sure there were others. Ron was the strong silent type. Slow, almost sloth-like, but keenly observant. I think they both enjoyed the adventures that total inebriation presents. Ron was a Vietnam veteran from the high, back country hills of North Carolina. He was functionally literate and strongly intuitive. I never traveled the heavy drinking road with them, but I knew the space and chose another.

My own Papa drank enough for all his nine kids.

What was I to Luther? I've thought that over many times during the sixteen years we knew him. It was Moanike'ala, Akaka—the Hawaiian Tigress—who shared with me the automatic recognition that this lanky, handsome, old, white-haired Hawaiian man was to become an intimate part of our family. He teased her, called her "the Queen of England" for her Scottish heritage. Moani was genuinely intrigued by his knowledge of things Hawaiian, especially genealogy.

To me it was the history of Hawai'i he carried in his person; it came from a uniquely authentic source. I first met Luther Makekau on Mamo Street. We somehow "connected". Suddenly from across the bar he barked at me in Polish. Startled, I barked back—"*Chazna Piva*" (time for beer), the only complete sentence I know in Polish. But we went along polishing our fake Polish to the astonishment of the regulars at the 50th State Bar in Hilo back in 1974.

"That's one crazy Ol man," I thought, soon as I recognized the old boy croakin' and croonin' in my kind of Polish—a pigeon Polish, for sure. *Chazna Piva* echoed again and this time Luther had the bar tendress set up the rounds. Everyone learned some Polish that afternoon.

Luther had learned his few words from the groups of 100 or so Russian and Polish immigrant workers enticed to the Islands by labor recruiters in China. The Poles and Russians were from mostly the middle and upper classes that left behind them the social upheavals of Europe at the turn into the 20th century. They were sold a bill of goods in part, sure of a place in the Island aristocracy, another ruling class position. Some of them were educated, white collar workers, upwardly mobile, free and adventurous. Luther worked and lived among them. Red was the big Russian he remembered best. It was Red, he said, who inspired the work crews to challenge and overcome their fears and to join him in working on building the Hilo breakwater.

Luther's idea of self should not be under-estimated. He was raised on John Wayne, Tom Mix, and Lash Leroux movies in his earlier years, and he was strong, very strong, all his long life; like a horse in heat. He'd shake your hand trying for the wince and plea for release—"I'm Luther!" Yet, he also knew of that other world beyond the ranch.

He was in part a product of what America brought culturally to Hawai'i, the Islands so recently stolen away. At various times I heard him roar and moan through his tears— "I'm a Maori!" And, if he had an audience, he'd trace his genealogy orally, proving one point or another. On other occasions he could be King Kahikili of Maui, a flag waving American, or a cantankerous ranch hand, beholding to no one. Always, if he was sober, you were sure to get a gentleman, like his parents raised him.

Luther liked to challenge and taunt people if it struck his fancy. And if someone challenged his reasoning, he'd find a reason to pick a fight—all this, unless, unless there was music in the air, in which case his rage would morph into some inebriated graceful *hula* rolls and turns, and he would insist you take the shirt from his back as a token of his Aloha.

"You and me Belsky," he'd crow, following his own logic, "we have the same disease—women."

I tell folks that if I knew Luther when he was in his prime, I'd have avoided him. He was Saint Lucifer to me—*Maka'ala!*

Beware!

Umi

11

Umikumamakahi

Luther's Birthday
July 13, 1890

When Luther was three years old America took over the Hawaiian Islands and his entire life was spent under the dual influence of an America coated Hawai'i and the remnants of one of the oldest cultures on earth. The Polynesian culture with its magic and pantheism proved no match for the monstrous waves of a foreign culture based on exploitation of the earth and labor under a strict plantation social structure. The relative serenity of the native people, when not indulging in and preparing for wars between local chiefs battling for control, was forever lost. Luther, at 83 when I met him, was still very much a terror on the streets, in the bars and boudoirs of Hilo and the entire Island of Hawai'i and beyond in fact; the women loved him, even as a broken octogenarian, cattle rustlin-cowboy must be loved. Now his powers were ebbing and he somehow knew it was his destiny to be a measuring stick for Hawaiian history and its place in the tomes of world history. He just missed the Viagra age and as he often repeated, "the ladies lose a lot when Luther fails to function."

But I digress.

Now his powers were ebbing. He was "Uncle Luther" to most; Luta to those who knew him intimately (and would chance the familiarity), and just plain Luther with a tinge of fear, respect and wonderment to everyone. He was known, often with a selected modifier ranging from *Kolohe* to *Kahuna nui.*

Luther's youth was strongly influenced by his grandfather who was the first non-*haole* missionary who came up from Tahiti with roots to the Maoris of Aotearoa—New Zealand. Luther knew of, and was fiercely proud of his warrior propensities often displayed when he would get "John Wayne-ish" if someone spoke critically about a cause he was championing—be it some nuance of Hawaiian genealogy or a criticism of America, or something he thought America meant to him. This was a very volatile loose cannon. In street language he was a subject "not to be messed with!" *Maka'ala* (watch out here comes Luther).

His Memory Lives On...
Come and Celebrate
Luther Makekau's Birthday with
"Eddie Kamae and The Sons of Hawai`i"
Music, Testimony & the first showing of the
5th documentary by Myrna & Eddie Kamae

Uncle Luther

July 11
two shows: 6 PM and 9 PM
at the
Pahoa Lounge
in Pahoa
Adm. $10.00

1890 - 1988

Hilo Quake

In the year of nineteen and seventy-five
the house gave a shake
a rock and a roll.

It was my first experience with earthquakes
save a slight nudge in San Francisco years before.
But this was a Pele slap
a wake-up call.

The baby was in her crib
Hawaiian Mama was up and with her
Before I got my bearings
Everyone's tutu, Uncle Luther,
rose from tending the garden.
"Ho," he called to us,
"some shake that, come one more
maybe bigger."

We stood there
mother, child and me
in the doorway
where it's supposed to be safer.
Thinking the tremor past I headed back to bed

Umikumamaha

the second jolt cut me off
just as Uncle Luther predicted
more powerful than the first.
"Outside, fast! Come!" Luther called.
We hurried down the stairs
into the expansive backyard.
The neighbors on both sides were already there
the Portuguese on our left
who never spoke to us
(we were referred to in their loud discourses
as the *haole* and the Hawaiian hippie *wahine*)
spoke through grey lips, perhaps to us,
"Some shake eh?"
"Oh yeah, hope the house doesn't come down,"
my Hawaiian Hippie *wahine* responded
somewhat automatically.
That was it
no more words.

Luther was bent over the taro patch
his sickle lifting and removing
a smile curled his lips
Moani and I saw it
neither of us understood
we were shaken but thankful
the baby was safe and the house still stood.

In an instant Luther bolted his six foot frame upright
"Come, we go upstairs,
listen to the radio

see what kine damage been done."
Upstairs we put on the radio
the local talk show
the cup of chatter was overflowing
"One light wen fall offa da wall."
"da books wen fall down offa da shelf."
"I wen fall down, twiss my knee one good one!
no can walk now, no can!"

"Ho! some jack asses, them," Luther scowled,
"dial up the station for me
I want make one report."
"No damage here, Luther," I said
"a few books, a dish or two—minor stuff."
"You dial em for me
I like talk with them."
Minor miracle I got through to the d.j.
"Hello, you're on the air"
Luther feigned hysteria—
"Ho, I wen hurt my back
the bloody house shake
throw me right off my neighbor's wife
some hurt for me,
I gettin' old already."

"Das you Luta?? You *Kolohe* you!
Why you no talk nice,
why you make I'dat?"
"Ho, Waltah, I no kid you—
I wen fall right offa da bed

an' da *wahine* no can hol me with da legs
das my neighbor's wife you know
an I already get 85 years, gettin old eh!"

"Luta you one *kolohe*
mo'bettah you stay Opihikao side
mo bettah fo you de'ah"

"Yeah, yeah, I go back home soon
but I jus reportin' the damage you know
good citizen *kine*, das me!"

"OK Luta, *mahalo* fo callin in,
you one *kolohe* buggah you
ahuihou."

Luther hung up the phone
had a gravel throated horse chuckle
put the tired straw hat over his silver locks
and shuffled out the door
down the steps
back to the garden.

Moani and I roared in appreciation.
The quake was over.

Princess Ruth Keʻelikolani was the embodiment of
Madam Pele and was, according to Professor Makekau,
genealogically connected to the fiery Goddess. Her rich
legacy has helped sustain the cultural survival and
renaissance of Hawaiʻi.

Cock Fight

In search of bananas at the market one afternoon, I saw Uncle Luther and Vicente, the friendly Filipino fisherman, in an animated discussion. Vicente was showing Luther the fine points of Grey, his fighting cock that had, according to the excited figure who stood about up to Luther's chest in height, won him a small fortune and was sure to continue his winning ways that afternoon at the Pepe'ekeo chicken fight. Luther insisted I join them as his guest. Vicente, whom I had just recently met, reluctantly agreed, for strangers at the illegal "Sport of Kings" are suspect.

Off the main road and into the abandoned cane field, cars were parked in no orderly fashion around a boarded, fenced-in arena with several men drifting about the entrance. After being visually scrutinized, I was allowed to enter as a guest of Vicente, Luther and Grey, who stood silently contemplating his own future from within a bamboo cage. Immediately upon entering my head went spinning with *déja vu* recognition of faces and places never seen before.

It was a local event, this chicken fight. I had seen cock-fights before in Mexico and Brazil, this Hawaiian-style event had a distinct Filipino flavor as our host Vicente, Luther's elderly friend, was quick to point out. This was apparently a family event from the number of women and children present. There were concessions with food and drink for sale. Youngsters, who

Vicenti's meal ticket
the Bad Rooster Grey

looked like my most disinterested math students, scurried about with dollars between their fingers and odds for bets fixed in their heads, a feat I would not attempt.

The red dirt arena or pit was perhaps twenty feet across with enthusiastic participants, mostly men, cheering on their prized birds and investments. There was blood, but it was not bloody. Why I cannot say. The birds that lost and died in combat were carried off and, I'm told, were consumed in rooster soup. A group of musicians played while people milled about in an ethereal setting. There were several card games and a dice game. Luther, who seemed to know everyone, mixed easily; I was cautious and kept a discreet distance, as Vicente had suggested.

After close to an hour, word spread that a police raid was going to take place shortly. Instantly the spell was broken, the bright colors and banners disappeared. Card games ended abruptly and like clockwork the gaming and festive acre of action became barren except for the few men who remained to satisfy the facade of law and order. Uncle Luther remained with a group of men as Vicente, with Grey tucked under his arm, ushered me into his tattered pickup and we sped off with the herd of other fleeing vehicles kicking up the red dust as we made our way back to Hilotown. The arena was transformed as is a theatrical stage set. In a matter of minutes the gathering of over fifty people became a skeleton crew of six, a couple of whom would be arrested, bailed out, and fined as penalty. Both Luther and Vicente took this totally in stride—standard fare for Big Island chicken fights.

Word of the impending police raid had cut short the scheduled fights. Grey would live to fight another day.

'DA WINNAH!'

Iwakaluakumamakolu

Iwakaluakumamaha

Luther's good time jail jamboree

HILO TRIBUNE-HERALD
A DAILY NEWSPAPER FOR
THE ISLAND OF HAWAII
HILO, HAWAII,
THURSDAY, SEPTEMBER 4, 1924
MAKEKAU,
BEERS AUTOS CRASH ON ROAD TO HONOKAʻA

Troubles do not come singly for Luther Makekau, former jailer at Honokaʻa who was a principal in the recent disturbance at the Honokaʻa courthouse. Monday morning while on his way to Hilo by automobile to obtain his pay from the county after having been discharged for alleged breach of discipline, Makekau met County Attorney W. H. Beers, who was traveling in the opposite direction. The meeting was very unexpected and, as it happened, at a sharp bend in the road near Kukaʻiau.

The suddenness of the meeting resulted in Makekau's automobile coming into contact with the front of Beers' machine in such a manner that both cars were damaged considerably.

Beers hailed a passing motorist who brought him back to Hilo, his machine being left on the road to be hauled to a nearby garage. Mekekau's machine was also put out of commission temporarily.

Beers and Makekau decided that neither driver was at fault, each sharing part of the responsibility.

Tuesday, Makekau proceeded to Hilo to collect his pay but, owing to the question which had been raised as to when Makekau ceased to be in the employ of the county, the pay

Iwakaluakumamaono

warrant was held up by the county auditor pending conclusive instructions from Sheriff Sam Pua.

Deputy Sheriff W. J. Rickard of Honokaʻa had previously said through the press that Makekau was discharged Monday, August 25, the day of the disturbance at the courthouse. Sheriff Pua had made a statement to the effect that Makekau's commission was canceled Tuesday, August 26. Makekau said Friday, August 29, that he had not yet been discharged and was still jailer on that date.

Makekau received a portion of his pay but there remains a small balance which is now available, Sheriff Pua having informed the auditor this week that Makekau's discharge was to date from the end of August.

This closes the matter on the same basis as was originally reported when Deputy Rickard was quoted as saying that Makekau would be discharged at the end of August.

HILO TRIBUNE-HERALD

A DAILY NEWSPAPER FOR THE ISLAND OF HAWAII

HILO, HAWAII, SATURDAY, AUGUST 30, 1924

WHO IS JAILER AT HONOKA'A?
IT'S YET A QUESTION

Is Luther Makekau jailer at Honoka'a or was he discharged Monday following the disturbance at the Honoka'a courthouse in which he is alleged to have been a principal?

This is the question The Tribune-Herald has been trying to solve since yesterday morning. Deputy Sheriff W. J. Rickard of the Honoka'a district insists that he dismissed Makekau last Monday. Makekau was reached by telephone yesterday noon and was equally insistant that he has not been dismissed.

Sheriff Rickard says Makekau is not the jailer at Honoka'a. Makekau says he is. Makekau is the son of Judge R. H. Makekau of the Hamakua court.

Sheriff Rickard says Makekau has been relieved of the keys to the jail. Makekau says he still has the keys in his possession.

Rickard said yesterday afternoon that Sheriff Sam Pua has appointed a new jailer, Henry Kahaliwai, to succed Makekau and that the new jailer assumed his duties last night. In a telephone message to The Tribune-Herald this morning Makekau said he was on duty at the jail yesterday and is working there again today.

The apparent misunderstanding arose following an account of Monday's disturbance at the Honoka'a courthouse published Thursday afternoon.

Visit Newspaper Office

Rickard and Road Supervisor W. C. Vannatta, accompanied by Supervisor A. M. Cabrinha, visited The Tribune-Herald office yesterday morning, Vannatta and Rickard to deny certain portions of the report published of the Honoka'a affair.

Rickard denied making any statement to the effect that Makekau would be dismissed at the end of the month, that he locked the jailer up after the latter had attempted to strike him, that the luau which Makekau is alleged to have attended had any connection with politics or that a number of police officers from adjoining districts were at the courthouse when the affair took place.

Rickard explained that his statement to a representative of the press was that he had dismissed Makekau immediately following the trouble at the courthouse Monday.

Vannatta denied making any statement to the effect that he was "running this district and would handle this affair." He explained that he was not so "swell-headed that I think that is true, much as I would like to run the district."

Cabrinha Not Interested

Cabrinha said he was not particularly interested in the Honoka'a affair.

After receiving Makekau's report yesterday noon in which he claimed he had not been dismissed The Tribune-Herald again got in touch with Rickard, who characterized Makekau as being "a liar if he says he was not fired."

Rickard then telephoned to the captain of police at Honoka'a who also said Makekau was discharged Monday. Rickard informed the captain that a new man had been appointed to take Makekau's place and to "tell Makekau his is *pau* and to get out."

Rickard also explained that Deputy Sheriff Solomon Larazo of South Kona was the only police officer from outside district who was present when the trouble occurred Monday. He said Lazaro brought the musicians from Waimea to Honoka'a.

Makekau insisted this morning that he did not see Rickard last night and that neither Rickard nor the captain of police had notified him that he has been discharged.

Still Doesn't Know It

"If I have been fired I'm sure I don't know anything about it," Makekau said this morning.

Makekau said he would come to Hilo tomorrow to "straighten things out." In the meantime the only answer to the question of Makekau's standing with the police department is that he was apparently discharged but does not know anything about it.

Most of all—Luther liked to have a Good Time!

93-year-old man is jailed in Big Isle threatening case

HILO — Luther Makekau, 93, of Hilo and Puna, yesterday was sentenced to five days in jail for his part in a dispute with a much younger man whom he had been accused of threatening.

Makekau, a retired Parker Ranch horse breaker, was charged initially with a felony count of terroristic threatening. But the prosecutor reduced the offense to second-degree threatening, a misdemeanor.

Makekau pleaded guilty and the judge sentenced him to five days in jail.

Makekau, believed by court officials to be the oldest defendant in Big Island cases, appeared several times in circuit and district courts over the last decade for fighting in bars. Once he was accused of cattle rustling — and he responded that he was the state's best rustler.

In November 1983, he spent a weekend in jail after a dispute with the owner of a Puna store.

At that time, his age was listed in court records as 85. However, in his latest scrape with the law, police and court records showed that Makekau was born July 13, 1890.

Kanakolukumamakahi

Luther's Grandpa

Uncle Luther would stay with Moani, the baby Erika and me for days, weeks and sometimes longer, when we lived above Hilo on upper Wailuku Drive back in the mid-70s. The police, being well acquainted with Luther for his numerous episodes outside the law, would simply deliver him to our door and help the usually inebriated old Hawaiian to his "corner" (his term) in the downstairs room. It was during these visits, especially the extended stays, that we benefited from his extensive knowledge of Hawaiian history, lore and practices—especially those areas related to plants, language and music.

During most of these visits Uncle Luther would either not drink alcohol at all, or have an occasional taste to keep lubricated. He would work the garden, make fish traps, create glistening *hula* skirts from the Hau tree, play a *ukulele* or write memories in his beautiful Palmer script handwriting. This was Luther's best side; in this condition he was a pleasant addition to our household. Such visits usually lasted no longer than seven days after which he would again be off to his other "homes" in Pahoa, Opihikao, Ka'u, Mamo Street in Hilo, or wherever the winds of fortune or misfortune deposited him.

I learned a lot about Luther from one particular extended stay. I remember the evening the police deposited Luther with us in an exceptionally unkempt condition. He was dead drunk, dirty, fouled beyond appreciation, and a complete mess. Having anticipated just such an eventuality, I had fashioned a device

Kanakolukumamalua

in the basement shower that allowed a shower spray to redeem him with a minimum of touching. It was after this unexpected appearance that Luther revealed to us a hitherto unknown aspect of his wild and wide ranging personality. It was, in fact, the longest unbroken stay Luther kept with us, and it would have continued indefinitely were it not for the transformation of his personality and the effect this alteration had on our household: Luther quit drinking—totally and absolutely. He also let his beard grow into a glistening radiant silver white. A snapshot of Uncle in this state is in Eddie Kamai's documentary- *One Kine Hawaiian Man.*

I encourage both these decisions and all was well and harmonious for the first three or four weeks. We learned during this time of Luther's grandfather, who he claimed was the first non-Anglo *haole* or white missionary in the Islands. This places him around the mid-19th century, a time of severe Biblical interpretation and religious fervor with attempts to apply Biblical pronouncements to domestic and civil conduct.

It was a time of chaotic social upheaval in Hawai'i. Perhaps it became fixed in Luther's DNA. "What a transformation," we thought. Luther sober and clean-cut was tantamount to a miracle. After about a month or so, I began to notice some changes. Luther's concern for things domestic had undergone a reformation: there was less music, a noticeable absence of singing and laughter and we noticed these black holes in our domestic universe.

Contradictions to our political thinking and activities were openly and often strongly advanced by this new squeaky-clean Uncle Luther. The missus and I tried to overlook these intrusions and did for another few weeks, but soon the pattern became such that the home atmosphere was becoming "uptight," our relaxed lifestyle became the focus of Uncle's super Puritanism and his transformed morals. Our housekeeping habits were, in his eyes, closer to Satan than God. Our language, which is transcultural and colorful, was condemned repeatedly. It was as if Luther's grandfather's two fisted fire and brimstone had been resurrected right in our home.

My Hawaiian activist wife was becoming uncomfortable in her own home. The goodhearted jocularity of the old Luther was no more! This new Uncle Luther poked barbed jams angrily at us, his hosts.

Something had to be done. We three discussed the situation and tried to draw some parameters that would maximize everyone's freedom of lifestyle. Luther apparently had become convinced of his unimpeachable position as *Pater Familias* of the household. I already knew what my ace in the hole would be, but had refrained from employing it. My own father had a serious romance with booze and I had adsorbed many a lesson, all well learned, on the vascillating vicissitudes of the behavior of alcoholics, be they inebriated or sober.

Late one evening I sat alone at the kitchen table with a deck of cards playing solitaire. On the table I placed a bottle of sherry—Uncle's favorite, and two empty glasses. Luther came in and sat opposite me. I glanced up and saw a crack in his new constitution as he noticed the sherry. I poured myself a small taste, downed it and wordlessly offered Luther the same. Without a hitch, he snapped up the glass, poured himself three fingers and drained it. That was it. We talked like the past several weeks never happened, shared some *pupus* and called it a night.

In the morning Luther was gone and didn't show up for a few more weeks. In the interim some friends from Ka'u came by and informed us that Uncle was in Ka'u, telling all who would listen that Tomas and Monanike'ala were subversives.

Law and Order Luther

One of the most important events of the 20th century in Hawai'i was the culmination of the labor struggle in Hilo on August 1, 1938. Luther was 48 years of age at the time. I asked him what he knew about those events that went on for several months and seriously divided the community. Being the son of a judge and territorial representative, he was a favorite son of the establishment although he broke every law on the books. The events of August 1, 1938 became known as "The Hilo Massacre." The ILWU, organized by Harry Lehua Kamoku, Yasu Arakaki and many others led a march on the Hilo docks to oppose strike-breakers the plantation bosses were sending in from Honolulu.

The sheriff deputized many men to oppose the peaceful marchers. Luther said he was an early volunteer to be deputized.

Shots were fired, no one was killed, but several were wounded and many injured in the melee that followed the confrontation. Film footage shows the scramble to avoid bullets and clubs. The strike was a major victory for organized labor in Hawai'i.

Mamo Street Ali'i

Labor Organizer Pepe Costa was driver for legendary labor leader Harry Lehua Kamoko

'Pico'
LIVING LEGENDS of HILO

Fred Nobriga (top)

Mamo Street, the soul of old Hilo and Makekau's talk story specialists; never a dull moment at the taxi stand.

Kanakolukumamaono

Kanakolukumamahiku

Uncle Luther Returns to Kahoʻolawe

The old man jumped out of the Zodiak landing raft into the rolling surf swimming and bouncing above the waves as he roared ashore amidst cheers laughter and awestruck adulation. First one ashore. Was he thinking of MacArthur in the Philippines?

"Luther has returned," he gasped, catching his breath, as he sat on the shore surrounded by fellow members of the Protect Kahoʻolawe ʻOhana (PKO), several of whom were one third his age.

"I was here in 1929," Luther calculated, "I was herding cattle for Parker Ranch, we fattened them up here before they went to Oʻahu. "That was some job! There was plenty grass here back then."

With an audience Luther did not shy away from his role as an elderly teacher or entertainer. "This island was a prison, you know, and wahines would swim or float over to visit their *kane*. Luther loved to tell stories and embellish details to keep the interest level up. He was like Mark Twain in that respect, not to be confined by the parameters of unblemished facts. There was no limit to Luther's enthusiasm for the position he now held as senior elder to the ʻOhana and their desire to reclaim, cleanse and nurture the Island for the Hawaiian people.

Kahoʻolawe was used as a practice bombing target since the onset of the Second World War in 1941, with the agreement that it would be returned to the people of Hawaiʻi upon cessation of hostilities. The war ended in 1945, but Kahoʻolawe continued to be the practice bombsite right up to the time of PKO landings. It was the ʻOhana led by George Helm, a musician; Dr. Emmett Aluli; and Walter Ritte—all from Molokaʻi—that challenged the legal and moral authority of the US Navy to bomb the Island. This heroic activity spawned the modern Hawaiian consciousness of *Aloha ʻAina*, a movement that has grown to this day (2015), with parallel movements worldwide based on the same universal principle of respect and *malama* (caring for) the Earth—mother of us all.

On the afternoon of the second day of the weekend occupation of Kahoʻolawe, Uncle Luther, who had kept busy and useful as an advisor and participant in construction of the *hale nui* (main house), called me aside and told me of a little joke he wanted to play on a couple of reporters accompanying the ʻOhana as well as any other curiosity seekers. At a given signal from the excited octogenarian, I was to lure the reporters and others to a cluster of bushes from which he would carry on. I agreed, and returned to my doodling, almost forgetting about Luther's plan. After several minutes I heard him hissing to me from behind a bush and fallen tree.

Luther's theatricality was here fully exploited. He had covered much of his rugged, handsome old face with charcoal black with traces of red around the eyes; placed upon his torn straw hat was a dried out goat's skull, embroidered with twigs, stones, bones and remnants of lesser critters. In his teeth he clenched a crude woodsman's knife. I did as was required. When the reporter and a few others came within ten yards of the bush,

Kanakolukumamaiwa

Luther sprang forth, roaring in his best gravel-throated base "Hey! What the bloody hell you doing on my island? I am the goat-man of Kahoʻolawe and I no need company here." then he switched into chanting in Hawaiian, gesticulating wildly.

With this everyone froze, startled and momentarily terrified by the unsettling and frightening sight of this bent over, ghost-like creature bouncing and bounding about in and out of the bushes. Had Luther not burst out laughing in appreciation of the success of his little joke, he could have milked a few more gasps and shrieks from the handful of his stunned audience. This was pure Luther, a thought-provoking jest among old and new friends. Something to remember him by.

We left Kahoʻolawe that next morning, cruised into Kihei on Maui and somehow lost track of Luther on the island of his ancestry through Kahikili, the great chief, said by some to be the father of Kamehameha the Great. Luther Makekau had many family members on Maui and he most certainly drifted into their lives most unexpectedly. We did not see him again until the police dropped him off at our door weeks later.

Kanaha

Kanahakumamakahi

Hula Skirt

One day Luther decided to make a *hula* skirt the way he had
learned years earlier—*Kahiko*—the old style. Two *hula* skirts
he would make one for Moanikeʻala and one for our infant
daughter Hoʻoululahui. He needed numerous branches and a
trunk or two of the *hau* tree, a native species that grew in a
grove just north of Hilo.

When we arrived at the designated location—a steep incline
that the *hau* trees leaned into—the eighty-five year old
Hawaiian became super energetic, giving me strict orders on
how to assist him. It was a hot day and my energy was sapped,
but Luther, more than twice my age, was super-charged. With
a coiled rope and machete attached to his person, Luther
grabbed a sturdy *hau* bough and swung off the incline, roaring
orders to me as to how to handle my end of the rope—slashing
away with his machete and dangling by one arm some twenty
plus feet above the base of the gulch. Fixing himself secure in
the thick wooded area, he cut the chosen limbs, tied them off,
and roared orders to me above to haul them up, untie the end
and return it to him for another round of the same. After a
seemingly endless repetition of this, Luther re-emerged anxious
to haul the *hau* branches and boughs into the pick-up. Cargo
secured, we returned home.

A large sink was filled with water to which bleach was added. The *hau* was stripped and set to soak in the bleach solution. After a while the strips were rinsed in fresh water and scraped clean, leaving a squeeky clean, slick, off-white strand between one and three inches wide. Again they were rinsed to get rid of all bleach traces. The result was a heap of beautiful *hau* strips, glistening off-white, that shimmered in the wind and sunlight.

Other strands he wove into a rope that held the vertical strips together. He deftly attached each vertical to the rope belt and the result was a splendid, sparkling *hula* skirt the likes of which is rarely seen today. Uncle Luther repeated the process and made the two skirts as promised, but they went neither to the intended recipients nor to some worthy museum or place of cultural preservation—Uncle traded them away for a bottle of sherry, promising to make replacements by and by. Unfortunately, that never happened.

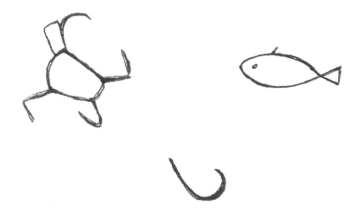

Kanahakumamaha

Red Luther

This is a story of Luther Makeau when he was both drunk and covered with lip stick plant (achiote). Now, when Luther had painted himself red—hair, arms, face, clothes—he was at the most ferocious of his numerous personalities, and for the most part, those who knew him got out of his way and made a special effort to avoid him, for when this lanky, aged, red-painted man with the flaming eyes was heading your way, it was an omen that trouble was coming.

One late afternoon Luther, painted red, came stalking down the lane unexpectedly, as he often did. I saw him coming and recognized right away that this was one of those times when Luther was not to be trifled with. I had been toying with an idea—a notion that perhaps music had the power to transform personalities. I thought this concept worth investigating and Luther, now ambling down the lane, might perhaps present a chance to try out my theory. Truthfully, while many people feared Luther when he was coated in red, I did not. I never did, perhaps this is because I had seen, and experienced the inebriated rage of my own father many times and for this reason it was not new to me, and I guess I just knew how to handle it intuitively. So, I calmly invited Luther into the house as he mumbled and grumbled his way up the dozen steps to the front door. Once inside, I sat him down and poured him a cup of

Luther on a bad night
was a formidable thing!
A Force — a force to behold...
and avoid.

Kanahakumamaono

iced *mamake* tea. I immediately turned on the record player and placed on the turntable an LP that we had gotten from the Bishop Museum in Honolulu—the collection of the history of music in Hawai'i. Luther and I had listened to the collection some time earlier, and I remember that when we played this music that had been popular in Hawai'i during the 1920s and 30s, it had sent the old Hawaiian into singing along and dancing to the catchy cha-langa-lang rhythms. It was naughty music that Luther recalled with a smile and an open laugh. It was music that was played when Luther was in his prime, perhaps twoscore years earlier. But this was Luther in red, a totally different personality.

I put the record on and played a couple of the oldest cuts on the album. Some of these old chants were actually recorded on the first recording devices—the Edison cylinders. I watched as Luther listened, but he wasn't really moved until we got into the more modern tunes—the *hapa-haole* songs with their catchy instrumental solos and clever multiple voice harmonies. It was this unique array of musical arrangements from the 20s and 30s that got Red Luther's foot to tapping and his fingers searching out a rhythm on the *ukulele* I had placed well within his reach moments before. He had fallen under the spell of the muse, first with a foot tapping and a light strum on the *ukulele* and finally with a constrained voice that soon became vibrant, clear throated and raspy, as must be expected from an octogenarian. Indeed, within a couple of minutes this terrifying old man—Red Luther—was being transformed into a *ukulele*-playing, foot-tapping, sing along, lovable Uncle Luther, and I recognize that there is, indeed, a transformative power in music. I was more than satisfied that my theory had worked out that evening. This transformed Luther washed the red from his body and had supper with us and remained for the evening

before disappearing again into the Hilo night. How conclusive can this experience be I cannot say, but it impressed me that if this potentially volcanic eruption of a man can be calmed by music, it's worth a try on every distraught soul. And I believe to this day, that not only music, but the Arts in general, can and must play a significant role in civilizing peoples everywhere to become self-fulfilled members of a national and global society. Indeed!   "Music hath power to calm the savage beast."
William Congreve (1670—1729)

Luther on a bench in Pahoa.

Pig's feet READY for the Pot.

Kanahakumamaiwa

Pigs' Feet and *Poi*

I guess, after deeper consideration, I can say that Pigs' Feet and *Poi* might be one way to envelop my damn near fourscore years on this planet. Between the Pigs' feet and the *Poi* lie the stuff these *pensamentos* (thoughts) are made of. I wish I could say they always rhyme—but that undermines the voice within—unless rhyme happens to be flowing with the message. That's another aspect of poetry—but here we are interested in pigs' feets and we'd best start at the beginning. I was minding my own business the other morning when the Poet Michelle phoned. "Belsky," he said, "please write me a poem entitled Pigs' Feet and *Poi*." After making sure I was hearing right, we had a laugh—a *carcaraja mesmo*—a deep throated horse laugh. Of course, we were both thinking Pigs' Feet (the hoof). So I've been thinking about Pigs' Feet ever since. Pigs' Feet was among Papa's favorite dishes and Mama cooked and jelled this stuff we called: *Kull-a-Jets*. Now this word, I thought, was a Yiddish word, but Jews have no truck with pigs' parts, so it must be from the Russian side of my blood ledger. My used-to-be Jewish Mother cooked the hoof of the swine for her husband Vasilli (Wally in America) and their nine dwarfs. *Kullajets* was eaten about once a month—usually in the brisk Jersey autumn or winter. I once ate so much *Kullajets* that I was dreadfully— very dreadfully sick for a week, and to this day I cannot look a Pig's foot in the eye without shuddering and reliving a seemingly continued desire to upchuck.

Kanalima

It all came about on a snappy, cold mid-winter night in New Jersey. It was close to midnight and I was anxious to run the five miles home after setting pins at the bowling alley for four hours. I felt good and ran at a good clip, seeing myself in a cross-country match with the leaders of the high school track squad. So I cut a good pace all the way home, running to the tune of my sneakers slapping through water and slush in rhythm to the latest blues tune spinning in my head. This carried me right up to my front door. And I was famished. There on the table sat a full tray—perhaps a dozen pieces—of pigs' feet—not quite jelled as Mama's pigs' feet were when at their best—but good enough for me with Little Richard jumping in my mind and a vacuum in the gut.

All through the house not a creature was stirring, so I set myself down and like the sorry pig that lost his feet, gorged myself. Three, five, perhaps seven Pigs' feets went down my gullet and I think I up-chucked one a day from that night forth. During the time under the hoof, so to speak, I became delirious, panicked and religious, swearing to that Last Resource never to eat another morsel of *Kullajetz*. Big Lesson there—just being healthy enough to eat, digest food and then have something to eat—that's double and triple blessings right there!

Well, Pigs' Feet slipped out of my life almost entirely—being reminded only when seeing them for sale from time to time in various cultural cuisines in ethnic communities. But I never tasted of pickled swine hoof again until perhaps fifty years later—the night I went carousing with my mephistophelian old Hawaiian friend Uncle Luther Kahikili Worthington Makekau, better known as Uncle Luther or just plain Luta, if you are willing to chance one of his untimely explosions.

Luther was in his late eighties and was a physical specimen that defied logic and the Ten Commandments. He was a hellraiser when he was in his cups and the white-haired high steppin' Hawaiian loved his sherry.

This particular evening Luther came by asking for a ride across town to a *pa'ina*—a party. With visions of Hawaiian music dancing in my head, I agreed to accompany him to the party. After a quick stop at the 50th State Tavern where he downed a glass of sherry and I fiddled with a beer for half an hour, he was ready. So was I.

Following Luther's hit and miss instructions we, after a few dead ends, pulled into a suburban lot on the outskirts of Hilotown. Keeping a bit of a distance, I followed the lanky, jovial cowboy up the driveway and into the festivities. A weekend *pa'ina* was underway beneath several tarps that extended the garage by a factor of three. After a few minutes of hugs, laughter, introductions and lapses into the Hawaiian language and what I call 'serious' pidgin, with the backslaps and eye-locks, I was properly presented to the gathered *'ohana* and immediately invited, mightily, to *komo mai e ai*—come, eat.

And what a spread lay upon the vast plywood table tops. There amidst flowers and decorations were the remnants of a turkey, a ham, and fish too numerous to mention among other Hawaiian delicacies. There in the center of the spread set the *'u meke 'ai*—a heroic wooden *poi* bowl. I've since learned that local folks have their unique ways of considering *Kanaka 'e*—a foreigner, as opposed to a *haole*—one without the breath of inner life or spirit. One of these aspects of consideration is how they relate to *poi*, for *poi* made from *kalo* or taro is the very brother to the *Kanaka Maole*—the Native, child of the Land.

Well, I had no problem eating lots of *poi*. I've loved it from the first—but it was the large tray of pickled pigs feet adjacent to the *poi* that made me shudder—I thought unnoticed, but no! A bright eyed lady, early into her cups for the evening, insisted I try the *poi* which I did, gladly, amid cheers and salutations. I had passed the test and was now part of an *'ohana* that held Uncle Luther as a sort of president emeritus. Having sampled and enjoyed a dish of *poi* straight, a full tray of baked fish and a pickled pigs foot was placed before us. Thankfully, before I could panic, Luther lifted the hog's hoof into his own plate, declaring it a vital assistant if "you go *holo holo*" (spend the night partying). The grease of the *wawai o ka pua'a*—pig's foot—coats the stomach with grease, reducing the alcohol that gets to the blood, and therefore, according to the First Book of Luther, you can drink a charming woman's husband under the table, enabling you, with your pig-foot-coated innards, to make off with the inebriated man's wife. This to Luther was sound advice he felt obligated to pass down to the next generation of lovers.

Well, that leaves me a long way from *Kullajetz* which started this little jaunt down memory lane, but in the end, I did taste a morsel of the pigs foot upon Luther's insistence, found it palatable, but not to become among my favorites. Recollections of culinary calamities die hard.

I passed the *poi* test with ease and actually overcame my dread of *Kullajetz* (by whatever name you call it—a pigs foot is a . . .) And even today I can greet a pig's foot with a smile or even a wink, should we notice each other in the world of culinary commerce.

*Gramatical exceptionalism and liberties have been employed in this tale.

The Poi Pounder

Kanalimakumamaha

Adventures with Luther

I

At 10:30 this morning I was told Luther was at the house looking for me to get fifty *ahi* (tuna) heads at the Suisan Fish Market. I went, saw the size of these fish heads and picked up eight twenty-pounders, went home, cooked two, froze three at grandma's, and gave three away. Luther came by at 1:30 to pick up another thirty-five to sell. We get to the market, the mass of heads is loaded along with many, many pounds of gizzards, livers, stomachs, and what all.

Luther now has a firm grip on my day. "Oh well," thought I, I hadn't run with him in a long time so I'm easy, too easy with the idea. We're off to take my loaded, rag-tag pick-up truck to Pahoa to sell our cargo to a community of Filipinos. But first we must stop at Luther's friend Mona's house.

We dump fish on her lawn and cover them with a rug and go inside. No one's home. Luther gets wine for himself and juice for me. Mona comes home, she knows Luther and wants no part of the fish. We reload, with considerable effort, the fish into the slightly fragrant truck bed. Mona is visibly relieved as we head off to see another "friend" to get a loan for gas money for the fourteen-mile trip to Pahoa to sell the fish parts.

I'm getting anxious to give them away. Luther protests, growling, "Nevah!" He's exhibiting the airs of an

Kanalimakumamalima

Kanalimakumamaono

entrepreneurial capitalist, a trait I'd never before observed in the old Hawaiian cowboy.

Now I'm writing, waiting for the 90 year old, semi-sober, wannabe capitalist to get the loan for gas money to carry the hundreds of pounds of fish residuals to the supposedly waiting Filipino fish-eaters in some hidden enclave in Pahoa. I'm trying to deny the reality of the fix I'm in: a hot day, a truck full of fish parts that are, apparently, not in popular demand. Luther insists there is a market just over the next hill in Pahoa. If not, they will be given away or dumped. I'm determined, for the flies are beginning to swarm and buzz.

I'm beginning to sense a Luther catastrophe. The old boy is no longer sober, but getting into his more normal state of inebriation. He is intense and energetic, but scattered in purpose, and the scheme is shifting against my better judgment after another stop and another few glasses of sherry. Luther's novelty scams, as he likes to call them, depend on others, most of whom, no, all of whom want nothing to do with Luther get-rich-quick capers.

I'm already stuck with the load of fish, stink and flies in my truck, and I'm already doubting the wisdom of going on this trip in the first place. Realization is upon me that I'd be lucky to extricate myself from Luther's grip by nightfall. I'm anxious to give the load away as fast as possible.

But I gave Luther the day, so I'm stuck with him and must now let things unfold as they will, fully aware that the load of fish will be a very nasty stinking mess in a few more hours. I must do as the Brazilians taught me—*Si Deus quizer*—if God wills it. And I sure hope God wills those Filipinos to want these free fish parts.

It has dawned upon me again that some of Luther's acquaintances call him Lucifer, jokingly; but the joke is going to be on me this day as the rains begin to fall and the daylight fades with my hopes of unloading the pungent cargo of fish segments and the inebriated nonagenarian. I have to retain my composure, for I walked into this one well aware of what it meant to *holo* (cruise) with Uncle Luther. This is going to be an all-nighter.

I thought back several hours to when, at home, I told Moani I was off to help Luther with some fish. She laughed and wished me luck, reminding me that I had just spent ten days in bed with a flu type bug. Luck rhymes with stuck, and that's what I was—stuck in a truck with a dead drunk Luther and a load of fast rotting fish in the bed, and the night descending as the rains turned torrential, sounding a lot like the gods having a good laugh as I squirm.

The illusion of selling or even giving the fish away vanished at the last stop in the mystical Filipino community. The men who did not quickly slide into shadows or hide at the sight of the lanky six-foot-two cowboy wobbling along in the mudd and downpour, smiled and laughed outright.

Luther disappeared into a doorway and reappeared a minute later carrying a bottle of sherry with a woman at his side. She grimaced as she grabbed a large fish head from the truck and quickly, without a word, dashed back into the open doorway. Uncle managed to get himself into the cab and his mumbling growls within minutes evolved into an uneven, arhythmic snoring.

The scenario was now complete and set: I was complicit in this scheme and now found myself the owner of this cargo of lunacy; my survival depended upon clear thinking and a systematic withdrawal from Luther's web. This was not my first ill-fated adventure with Luther, and I vowed it to be my last, IF I made it out of this one, for one never knows where or how things are going to wind up hitched to Luther in his cups. Trying to put a positive spin on things, I thought things could be worse, but I did not know how. This I was to learn forthwith.

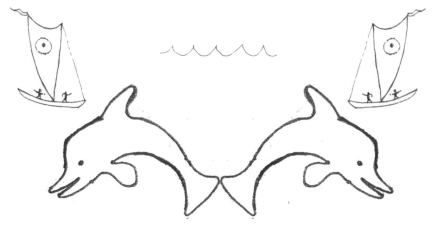

II

When you don't know what to do, do nothing. So I sat in the driver's seat and listened to Luther's staccato snoring, in and out of time with the gods pounding their raucous laughter on the cab roof. Knowing I could not sleep, I surrendered to the darkness that consumed me in and out of the truck.

After a mini-lifetime the rain slackened and I decided to take the situation in hand. The first issue was to get rid of the fish, the longer they remained in the truck the more disastrous the odiferous consequences. But how? First choice was to get them dumped into the ocean, but no fisherman would want this stinking cargo in his vessel now or in the morning. Next choice: bury them—but where? I was carrying a truckload of rich fertilizer when viewed from the positive side; a load of powerful stench from the negative. "Think positive," says I to meself, and Malu 'Aina came to mind instantly.

Malu'Aina is the Center for Non-violent Peace Activism run by taro farmer Jim Albertini in Ola'a (Kea'au) just ten or so miles ahead in the dark, rainy night. Jim was away for a few weeks and had asked me to "watch the farm" in his absence. After a few days of living in the raw environs of an abandoned cane field, working in constant rain, living in a tent and working the 'aina planting bananas and sweet'taters in the lumpin mudd, I fell ill with what I thought was the flu, but turned out to be lepto.

It was from this illness that I was mending when along came Luther. And here am I, trying to see the dark, rain soaked road to Malu'Aina, and, hopefully the end of this most distressing misadventure. Uncle Luther was now asleep at my side, mouth widely ajar, with his lonely main tooth so visible and the contented wisp of a smile on the ageless wrinkled "map" of an overgrown *menehune* who I knew could be an unmanageable demon on a bad night.

What might I expect upon reaching the farm? I remembered that there were no toilet facilities—outhouses were the first necessities to be met following Albertini's instructions. Perhaps the Hawaiians and other members of the Aloha 'Aina Peoples' Party had made some progress; or, perhaps the constant rains and mud had dampened their revolutionary fervor and the ways of the flesh had overwhelmed them. This, thought I, as I managed the perilous trip from Pahoa to Ola'a that rainy night. Luther slept on, wheezing, and giving an occasional yelp which both startled and gave me to smile—a break in an otherwise dismal situation.

Malu'Aina is another vehicular venture of mudd and puddles. The pitch black, overcast night was cut only by the lantern barely aglow in the main tent at the end of the cane field. Two of the residents wobbled to the tent entrance as we approached and proved to be sober enough to help me get "Uncle" to a readied cot. After I explained the need to empty the truck that very hour there was an incredulous expression on the faces of the brothers so unfortunate as to be awake at the time. They eyed their mates, asleep, wasted to the world: "We get a drunk Uncle Luther and the task of shoveling a load of stinking fish in the rain," was obviously churning in their heads. It turned out to be that bad, perhaps worse, depending on the level of one's psychic masochism.

For me it was a wondrous relief—the first step toward disentanglement from Luther had been accomplished. My strength was being sapped away and I feared a setback—both mental and physical—but my burden had been eased and I could now get back home to sleep and figure out the next step,

Kanaonokumamakahi

Two of the residents wobbled to the tent entrance

Kanaonokumamalua

which was to hose down the truck before the fish guts gave forth their unique odor to the coming day. But I made it home, dragged myself into the shower and then to bed after a brief nod of understanding to *miwahine* and went down for the count.

"Eat when you're hungry; sleep when you're tired; work when you can," words of wisdom passed on to me from my doctor's grandmother.

The next morning began in the mid afternoon. The truck was a foul smelling object of curiosity to the neighbors who watched in puzzlement as the *haole* artist sped away in his fish-stink vehicle. I must have left a foul trail of stink and flies as I whisked through town and out to the farm intent on burying the fish and ending this caper that had taken me away from my studio and the paintings bursting in my head at the time.

The farm was secondary to me; art was first, it is my weapon with which to fight injustice and oppression, it's the only one I have confidence in to carry my will, my vision to others. If everyone did their best at what they do best, the world becomes a better, a happier place for everyone. What better place to begin such a revolution than Hawai'i? A land blessed with all the raw ingredients for a paradise on earth. If I plowed into this farming effort, surely the other guys and girls would follow. Together we could create an example for the community to follow. This I knew to be dancing with fantasy—a residual of Peace Corps brainwashing that evolved into an idealistic, quixotic life style.

The gang on the farm was almost to the one, local, young men who had the history of the Islands written in their lives and idiosyncrasies: Honolulu's own dispossessed, landless, coming from crime and drug ridden environs, drastically aborted

Kanaonokumamakolu

education and a rich resume of correctional institutions—the real deal—the salt of the Earth—*Maka'aina*.

Luther was bent over tending the fire with a fork, poking it around beneath a relic of a western movie coffee pot. "The Nation," that's what I called the gang, was mostly awake, stirring groggily around the kitchen tent, mostly in silence except for Luther's growling about the lazy *lapuwale* (ne'er-do-wells) that had given him comfort the night before. They all knew Luther. The old rustler was ridiculed and teased; and equally they feared him. For when he was serious and sober, Luther was a most respected elder, his knowledge of the language and culture were unchallenged by the leaders of the Hawaiian aristocracy. But those precious moments were diluted and polluted by the more devious of his numerous personalities.

Luther showed no sign whatsoever of the past night's inebriation, but he did look like an explosion waiting for an opportunity to cut loose. I recognized this and turned the conversation to music and Uncle's good old days.

Two volunteers joined Luther and me. We made our way across the mudd-puddled grounds to the banana patch where we had discharged the cargo of rotting fish the night before. The smell was horrendous and getting worse by the minute. A swarm of flies hovering over the mass of putrid fish was revoltingly fantastic. It was agreed that the fish had to be buried, but we had not anticipated the difficulty of digging holes sufficiently deep in the rock strewn banana patch. Getting to a depth of one foot was a major accomplishment and I knew that a depth of double that would be minimal to quell the smell and keep dogs and critters from disinterring the remains, thereby prolonging and complicating an already revolting situation.

Several of us worked through the remainder of the daylight and the clouds of flies until we had covered, but not buried the fish. Digging proved so difficult that we lowered the bar of acceptability to the degree that by nightfall a mass of the mess was simply covered with banana leaves, believing the flies would have to work harder to get to their target. Exhausted, we laid down our shovels and picks and dragged ourselves back to the kitchen tent where a couple of *wahines* had cooked up some potatoes with spam and bananas.

After washing up at the one water outlet then available, we sat around and talked about the business at hand. The outhouse that had been built in an area that was directly in line with the main entrance, would have to be moved, but to those who had dug the hole, again no easy chore, their plan for the farm was quite different from what I had envisioned, which was different again from what Albertini envisioned and proscribed. There was no main plan at this early stage of the peace center, and the absence of the leader meant there were serious problems as to where to put the essential structures—the privies being foremost on this list.

After supper the *ukuleles* appeared, the libations distributed and friendly bantering which invariably ended in abusive behavior of a generally non-violent nature. Uncle Luther was now fully incorporated into the group and his cantankerous nature did little to build a sense of community among the tent dwellers. Weakened by the day's effort, I made off in the stinking truck to Hilotown where I could luxuriate in a shower, de-aromatize and get my much needed rest.

The adventure with Uncle Luther was almost over; one more day at the farm, a half day or so to clean the truck again, and the final visit to the fish heap yet to be covered, and that was about all I could hope for. Albertini was due back in a few days and I was anxious to get my own life back on track.

The sun was sinking fast into the last of the rain clouds when I made it to Malu'Aina the next day. The fish heap in the banana patch was as we had left it the night before; no one had made an effort to address the problem that day. The horrendous odor now was powerful in the surrounding area of the farm and beyond. I found Luther sitting alone in a corner growling to himself in reference to the *lapuwale*. After talking story for awhile we walked toward the banana patch despite the stench, and under a moon nearly full I saw the fish carcasses that had been dragged about by dogs and night critters. In total distress, I looked at Uncle Luther and saw the moon reflected in his *kahuna* eyes. Closer inspection revealed the sluggish movement of many, many maggots upon the exposed fish remains, these too were dancing in Luther's eyes in the moonlight. The old cowboy had an other-worldly smile on his face.

The farm and the surrounding area would have to ride out the stench. My continuing in this battle was tantamount to suicide from my new, realistic point of view. Even today, these decades later, I still see the face of Uncle Luther, a self satisfied grin and glazed eyes reflecting the fish caper in the moonlight. Jim Albertini alone can write the concluding portion to this mis-adventure, for he too was carried into the swirling currents of an adventure with Uncle Luther. I hope Jim writes it, for travels with Luther have no fixed end.

"Everyday that doesn't kill you, improves you!" a self proclaimed messiah once told me. I am much improved.

Kanaonokumamaono

Last Round Up

Now, dear reader, we have a sketch of this Luther man. A few questions come to mind, questions that have been presented to me by others who have met Luther and knew not what to make of him. Was Luther a Christian man? Luther could give a powerful *Pule* (prayer) before a meal. These were always in Hawaiian and always solemn, understood by few present. Luther's idea of a Heaven and a Hell are well documented in the film by Eddie Kamae. We see Luther toward the very end of his life, well lubricated and in a mellow space; to paraphrase his words: "Listen my children, I am soon to be judged by *Ke Akua o Ka Lani* . . .almighty God; if I go up above, well that's very good and I will signal to you in spirit—Come!"

"If I go down below into the Fire—Stop, Don't Follow . . .Don't follow." This is the heartfelt Luther—concerned for the world.

I think he was amazed that he had lived so long. There were times when he longed to be with his generation(s), times when he was vital, energetic, "a rustler, a Lover and a rough Jack." In his universe the ashes of his fiery days roared on in his dancing man's mind. The times in Pahoa and Kea'au when he would strip down, damn near naked, to dance with a free spirited woman, often bringing the police to calm the subsequent uproar. Luther just missed the Viagra era, perhaps for the best for all of us of both sexes.

The night Gabby Pahinui died, Luther wept. His tears were not only for the passing of this giant of Hawaiian music, but also for the fact that he would have loved to leave this world on the same day. He felt left out, hurt by the powers that he always felt guided his life. Luther was tired and weakened by his long journey through life. He had a strange, very personal relationship with his God; he lived and died with big questions left unanswered.

The happiest Luther I remember was when we had a spacious quarter with a spare room that was his "corner." In contentious moments he'd scowl, "You stay in you corner; I stay mine."

With his hands working the earth Luther was one with the *'Aina* (land-spirit), clear headed and wise. When he was part of a group of accomplished musicians he was a contagion of Joy and Good Times. He was complete and happy as a cowboy and even a scholar and teacher. There was nobility in his savage soul and alcohol fueled him along for most of his 99 years. Sherry was Luther's lubricant of choice. I remember sharing a joint—*pakalolo*—with the old boy among a circle of friends on a few occasions. He never smoked tobacco but chewed the old, coiled, black rope tobacco, using it as a weapon to "blind" an opponent in a fist-fight. Hopefully this was more braggadocio than fact.

He approached a challenge as one of his idols would—could be John Wayne or Tom Mix—tough good guys. If sober he would be diplomatic, leaning on the good advice of his father, a judge and Territorial Representative. Luther's "good guys" were made in Hollywood, carefully sifted by theatre owners in the newly annexed Islands. These were the years of extreme Americanization of the Hawaiian Islands in law, patriotism,

'Ohana

Kanaonokumamaiwa

language and religion. Hyper-patriotism reigned in Hawai'i during the two World Wars as political propaganda was rampant around the world and the Islands were no exception.

When Luther Makekau passed away in 1989, he was an acknowledged historic relic of an age long since faded. The world had morphed into an enigma of modern conveniences, gadgets and contrivances. His century long life was filled with the most astounding advances of "civilization" in human history, and Luther in his unique, strong-willed manner managed to challenge the tsumani of "Progress" by asking and living the big question: What is a good life according to man's nature?

Shakespeare gives us Falstaff; Hawai'i gives us Uncle Luther.

"What is 'Ohana?" I once asked Luther as we were both relaxing in hammocks on a warm afternoon. This was the type of question Luther, sober and clean-living as he was at this time, loved to answer, to paint with words: "It's a precious, a sacred word, and when understood is carried in the soul."

Glossary of Hawaiian words

ahi . . . . .tuna
ahuihou . . . . .til we meet again
Aloha ʻĀina . . . . . . .spiritual connection to the earth
hale nui . . . . .main house
haole . . . . .foreigner, stranger, White, American,
                    caucazoid
holo holo . . . . .to cruise
Holo kūkū me . . . . .trot or gallop along with
hoʻokupu . . . . .sacred offering
hula . . . . .dance
Kahiko . . . . .old style
Kahuna . . . . .priest, expert in any profession
Kanaka ʻe . . . . .stranger, foreigner, heathen
Kanaka Maole . . . . .native person
Kane . . . . .man
Kolohe . . . . .rascal, jester, trouble maker, rogue
komo mai i ai . . . . . .come eat
kumu . . . . .teacher, foundation
lapuwale . . . . .neʻer-do-well
mahalo . . . . .my spirit thanks your spirit
Makaʻaina . . . . .salt of the earth
Makaʻala . . . . .beware, keep your eyes open
mālama ʻĀina . . . . . .care for the earth
menehune . . . . .mythical little people similar to leprechaun
nui . . . . .big, to intensify
ʻohana . . . . .extended family, related or not
pakalolo . . . . .marijuana
paʻina . . . . .party
poi . . . . .delicacy of Polynesian diet (made from
                    cooked and pounded taro corms)
pule . . . . .prayer
pupu . . . . .appetizer
ʻu meke ʻai . . . . .poi bowl, source of food
wahine (mi-) . . . . . . .woman (my)
wawai o ka puaʻa . . .exuberance of grease from a pig's foot

Kanahikukumamakahi

Aloha ʻĀina

Born of the *Protect Kahoʻolawe ʻOhana* now part of an
international movement to protect and care for the earth

Almost forgotten in Hilo's rush to the modern is Nawahi Lane located between Mamo and Ponahawai Streets off Kamehameha Ave, named for Joseph and Emma Nawahi, founders of Ke Aloha 'Aina , nupepa—a newspaper for Hawaiian Loyalists and persons opposed to the overthrow of The Hawaiian Kingdom of 1893. Joseph Nawahi understood Hawai'i's place in the tumultuous changes "Manifest

Destiny" brought to world politics. Understanding and comfortable in both Hawaiian and American cultures, he served as the Queen's Representative on the Island of Hawai'i and was an attorney, educator and outstanding orator, he was perhaps the most polished and charismatic personality of his day. He was a devoted confidant of his Queen, Lili'uokalani, serving as her emissary to the US in Washington DC.

Joseph Nawahi

Emma Nawahi

Ke Aloha Aina kept the kanaka maoli informed as to the state of the Queen and Hawaiian affairs during the dark daysze following the insurrection. The newspaper was published faithfully until 1920 by Emma Nawahi after Joseph's death in 1896

In winter of 1981 The Protect Kahoʻolawe Ohana published an issue that updated the newest gencration of Aloha ʻAina Patriots to the necessity of defending Kahoʻolawe from being bombed by the US military, and the ruinous consequences of over-development in Hawaiʻi, and the sad state of the Kanaka maoli in health, incarceration and education.

The editorial staff of Aloha ʻAina Ea Ea, the latest incarnation of the nupepa, is dedicated to the same goals as those of Joseph K. and Emma Nawahi back in 1895—to promote PONO in Hawaiʻi.

Ua Mau ke Ea o ka ʼAina I ka Pono.
The Life of the Land is perpetuated through Righteousness.

1895

PUBLISHED BY THE PROTECT KAHO'OLAWE FUND • P.O. BOX H, KAUNAKAKAI, MOLOKAI HAWAII 96748   WINTER 1981

1981

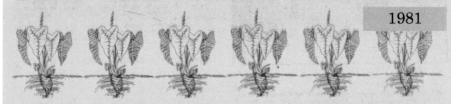

KAHO'OLAWE: A NATIONAL HISTORIC MONUMENT

Pule

Aloha no ka po'e Hawai'i, malihini, and
people who love Hawai'i Nei,
Most gracious Heavenly Father, Mother,
Sisters, and Brothers,
And all the gods that have come
to our shores, who have thrived in our love,
Whose people have inter-married with our people,
And shared our culture, our tears and our
laughter until there were no differences,
Our destiny became one.
Listen and read the words of the many:
the opio, napua, kupua, kupuna,
and the kumu of our cherished love.

Hewa

The Protect Kaho'olawe 'Ohana recently just learned that the Keeper of the National Register has determined that the entire Island of Kaho'olawe is eligible for listing on the National Register of Historic Places. This determination gives national recognition to the position long-held by the Protect Kaho'olewe 'Ohana; that the entire Island is significant.

As early as January 4, 1976; the Protect Kaho'olawe 'Ohana had stated that the Island contained archaeological sites of importance to the native Hawaiians and to the cultural heritage of the nation. Not until ordered by the United States District Court in the Aluli v. Brown lawsuit did the Navy commence to comply with the law by beginning to survey Kaho'olawe for archaeological sites. After nearly four years, the archaeologists have discovered five hundred forty-four sites which together disclose the cultural, religious, subsistence, political, and settlement patterns of the early native Hawaiians. As the first, and probably only, island-wide survey of such intensity, the findings provide a unique opportunity to illuminate the Hawaiian past. By treating the Island as a whole entity, an archaeological district rather than individual sites, the Keeper of the National Register has validated the position of the Protect Kaho'olawe 'Ohana that the entire Island is culturally and religiously significant.

The State Historic Preservation Officer, Susumu Ono, after obtaining recommendations from the Board of Land and Natural Resources and the Hawaii Historic Places Review Board, had recommended to the Keeper that the entire Island of Kaho'olawe be listed on the National Register. Similar recommendations were made by Lt. Governor Jean King, Mayor Hannibal Tavares, Hawaii's Congressmen and the Society for Hawaiian Archaeology.

By determining Kaho'olawe eligible for listing on the National Register of Historic Places, the Keeper has provided continuing protection for this cultural, religious and educational resource of our nation. The Navy must consult with the Advisory Council on Historic Preservation regarding all military actions on Kaho'olawe that would adversely effect the archaeological sites. The purpose in mandating that the Navy must consult with the Advisory Council is to insure that the Navy considers feasible and prudent alternatives to military actions that would adversely effect the archaeological sites on Kaho'olawe and, thereby, avoid adverse effects on this cultural, religious and educational resource of our State.

With this national recognition of the significance and importance of Kaho'olawe to our nation's cultural heritage, the Protect Kaho'olawe 'Ohana's firmly held belief in **aloha 'aina** (love of the land) has received national support and validation.

Our Newspaper

today

We dedicate this newspaper to the spirit of Aloha 'Aina, our traditional Hawaiian value system: to love the land and to protect the land for the present and future generations of Hawai'i's children. The original Ke Aloha 'Aina newspaper's home was Hilotown. It was published by Joseph Nawahi, a beloved true Hawaiian patriot, teacher, lawyer, writer, artist, twenty-year legislator, member of the cabinet and trusted advisor to Queen Lili'uokalani as well as her Minister of Foreign Affairs during the last months of the Monarchy. Nawahi and his wife Emma 'Aima helped to found the Hui Aloha 'Aina political party. They worked tirelessly to restore Hawai'i's independence as a nation and to stop annexation to the U.S. He was imprisoned in 1895 for acts deemed treasonous by those who had stolen the Kingdom. During his incarceration he contracted tuberculosis which led to his early death in 1896. His wife continued the newspaper and helped organized the famous petition against annexation.

Tee Shirt Prints

by

tomas

Paintings

Prints

Poetry

Books

TomasBelsky.com

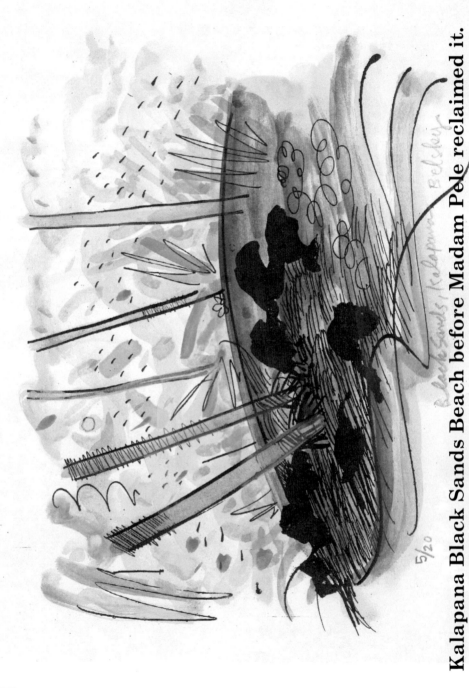

5/20

Black Sands, Kalapana Belcher

Kalapana Black Sands Beach before Madam Pele reclaimed it. One of Uncle Luther's comfort zones in Puna district.

'Tis said that through the exploration of language one discovers the soul and spirit of its speakers. Here's an example recently stumbled across:

There's a certain water dwelling critter called, in the vernacular English, the "Speckled Parrot Fish." The scientific or Latin name of the same fish is "Chlororus Perspicitatus Steindachneer, 1879".

The Hawaiians, amongst whom said creature dwells, call it "Ahuʻula,"

and its lover is called "Uhu uliʻuli."

Now, which would you rather dance to?

Famous and notorious Mamo Street
in the heart of old Hilotown.

History

We are born
And find ourselves adrift
In the turbulent seas
And tides of History.
We are carried along
And we cling to that which
Keeps us afloat
A sturdy ship
A log a raft
A fancy yacht.

Beyond our capacity to control
Are the waters around us
Angry and opaque
Calm and clear
Into which we can perceive
Many mysteries and beauties
Of these Waters of Life

Some are swept away early
By storms and events
That rise and fall by powers
We have come to understand
But not control
And we must stand in awe
Of the majesty of the unknown
Despite the pains and sorrows
The joys and exaltations.

If that which sustains us
Gives us life across years
We come to understand
If we are blest with
The capacity to understand
That there may yet be method

To the madness.
(or not).
As the pieces to our puzzles
Are laid out before us
Examined and joined together
To contribute to the completion
Of a more grand design
Than we are privileged to
comprehend
As comprehension allows.

And there are those
Who have come to confirm
The dreams of those who sailed
These seas before us
That our vessel too
Must one day touch a land
Of our dreams
At journey's end—
which is not an end at all
But a step into another
beginning
Where that which confounds us
Comforts us
In our return to the Dreamtime
From whence that tide of
History
Has carried us
And perhaps we meet again
All those who sailed
In earlier times
Across other tides and climes.
And Yes—
    (maybe not)
                Fin   4:25 AM

Spinning True

We must relearn that we are all
All spokes in a delicate wheel
Whose point of perfection is to spin True
A perfect circle in spinning
Rubbing neither the left nor right side
Of the supports
To be out of harmony
Too loose or too tightly adjusted
Distorts and impedes the purpose
Of the wheel itself
Each spoke is part of the perfection
Responsible for its own true tension

And there's V. Mayakowsky
His Poet's analysis of the bureaucrat
In the person of the tax collector:
Professional inferiority complex
Insignificance and ambition
Always need someone to deride
It's not a new phenomenon,
But the modern has made it a threat
To all we know as our noblest aspect.

They said of Carl Sandburg
"Only a child of immigrant parents
Could see America
The way he saw her."
I'm another of those
And I feel America much
More than I see her
For I live in the last colony
Of Her earlier stage of
Manifest Destiny.

Luther's Mamo Street Haunts

EEH! YOU GOOSEFUKKAMYAHGOOSENAROOF!!

The Joys of Retreat

One retreats when it is
considered both
wise and prudent and
furthers the Grand Design.

What has survival got to do
with it?
If Love is not at the root
of the tree we plant
the fruit can only be bitter
and not worthy of the
martyrs' sacrifice.
Getting into Heaven is
one thing
Getting out another?

Why might one want to
leave 'Heaven?'
To experience ecstasy
as we know it?

Your Paradise so narrow
too dank, dark and shallow

Mine is quite the opposite
My throne lies on an Angel's
Breast
and a cello plays
each days sunset.

Ah yes, I know
that sweet refrain

I've heard it before
and I'll hear it again.
'You dance with
the Angels
on the head of a Pin,
have a really good time
and there ain't no sin."

   Yes!
sinnin's for critters
like me down below.
The pitch is fast
But the curve is slow.

E hulimana'o Brother
it's never too late
St. Peter will greet you
at the Gate.
With a Blonde and a Redhead
and two raven haired beauties
to reconnect your soul
their solitary duty.
There ain't no work
and there ain't no pay
no need for nothin
but to love each day.
Don't measure Heaven by
the rules down below
Hulimana'o Brother
Let the Good Times Roll.

Strongest Muscle in the World

Street wisdom
Learned from a home boy on Mamo Street
Big Keoni was being overly exuberant
   His exploits as line-backer
    A decade and a hundred pounds lighter ago
    Again he relived the bulging muscles
        As he smashed into the quarterback
           Tossing him for a ten yard loss.
Curvaceous and delicate
She waltzed in
Covered all of us with her smile
Pointed only at him
And placing him securely under her thumb
Sashayed out
He was still exhorting and pontificating
   But incoherent now.
 Homey smiled and smacked his lips
      poeticizing . . .
"The strongest muscle in the world!"

On Painting

Why do your think Winston Churchill
and Dwight Eisenhower anticipated
and loved their solitary hours
with brush, color and palette,
doing full combat
against an adversary within?
  —having lived through hell
    they take, need a break.
But where do Souls
like Eisenhower, Churchill,
Washington and Castro,
Mao and Mickey Mantle,
Stalin and Jackie Robinson
Where can these lofty souls escape to?
Hours of meditation will get you there,
    but Painting is a short-cut
Perhaps, just perhaps its a way
Through these self-made
Soul Droppings
    to examine the self.
and Miles. . . is he a Painter?
What is Miles after
trumpeting himself the modern Primitive
    yes!
When the Great ones take to Painting
where do Painters turn?
Up the road
    to Miles
    Left on Mayakowsky.

Poets' Rule

More and more
information floods the mind
Radio, TV, cable news
Religiously tainted
   Pontificated
       Latest news
Bruised news
   round the clock decaffeinated
Anonymously authenticated news
News of the news
   news you can trust
news of the wars
news of lust
   News of global calamity
and balls in the rough.
Blues news, bad news, no news
—too much is enough.

Give me some good news:

The cop smiled at the hippie
   As he lit a joint,
the cat smiled at the passing dog
   and curtsied appropriately;
the banker approved the loan anyway!

Something big is happening now –
something very big
and long overdue:
Rule of the
"Cloud Dwellers" *

****
Stalin referred to Pasternak and his ilk as "Cloud Dwellers."

The Award-Winning Hawaiian Legacy Series

HAWAI'I INTERNATIONAL FILM FESTIVAL AUDIENCE CHOICE AWARD

LUTHER KAHEKILI MAKEKAU

A One Kine Hawaiian Man

A documentary by Eddie & Myrna Kamae

... Deals with one of Hawai'i's real characters ... a fascinating story ...
– Dave Donnelly, HONOLULU STAR BULLETIN

"Plant something every day."

Luther

43761606R00062